In the name of Allah
The Merciful, the Compassionate

Presented to ....

....

From ....

Date ....

Other Goodword books on Islam

- Tell Me About the Prophet Muhammad
- Tell Me About the Prophet Musa
- Tell Me About the Prophet Yusuf
- Tell Me About Hajj
- A Handbook of Muslim Belief
- The Moriscos of Spain
- The Story of Islamic Spain
- Spanish Islam
- A Simple Guide to Islam's Contribution to Science
- The Quran, Bible and Science
- Islamic Medicine
- Islam and the Divine Comedy
- Decisive Moments in the History of Islam
- My Discovery of Islam
- Islam At the Crossroads
- The Spread of Islam in the World
- The Spread of Islam in France
- The Islamic Art and Architecture
- The Islamic Art of Persia
- The Hadith for Beginners
- Islamic Thought and its Place in History
- Muhammad: The Hero As Prophet
- A History of Arabian Music
- A History of Arabic Literature
- Ever Thought About the Truth?
- Crude Understanding of Disbelief
- The Miracle in the Ant
- Allah is Known Through Reason
- The Basic Concepts in the Quran
- The Moral Values of the Quran
- The Beautiful Commands of Allah
- The Beautiful Promises of Allah
- The Muslim Prayer Encyclopaedia
- After Death, Life!
- Living Islam: Treading the Path of Ideal
- A Basic Dictionary of Islam
- The Muslim Marriage Guide
- A Treasury of the Quran
- The Quran for All Humanity
- The Quran: An Abiding Wonder
- The Call of the Qur'an
- Muhammad: A Prophet for All Humanity
- Words of the Prophet Muhammad
- An Islamic Treasury of Virtues
- Islam and Peace
- Introducing Islam
- The Moral Vision
- Principles of Islam
- God Arises
- Islam: The Voice of Human Nature
- Islam: Creator of the Modern Age
- Woman Between Islam and Western Society
- Woman in Islamic Shari'ah
- Islam As It Is
- Religion and Science
- Tabligh Movement
- The Soul of the Quran
- Presenting the Quran
- The Wonderful Universe of Allah
- Selections from the Noble Reading
- Heart of the Koran
- Muhammad: A Mercy to all the Nations
- The Sayings of Muhammad
- The Life of the Prophet Muhammad
- History of the Prophet Muhammad
- A-Z Steps to Leadership

Concerning Divorce

Maulana Wahiduddin Khan

Goodword
B·O·O·K·S

First published 2001
Reprinted 2002, 2003, 2008

No Copyright
This book does not carry a copyright.
Goodword Books gives its permission on reproduce this book in any form or to translate it into any language for the propagation of the Islamic cause.

Heavy discount is available on bulk purchase of this book for distribution purpose:

The text in this book is gleaned from
Islam Rediscovered by Maulana Wahiduddin Khan

Goodword Books Pvt. Ltd.
1, Nizamuddin West Market, New Delhi - 110 013
email: info@goodwordbooks.com
www.goodwordbooks.com

Printed in India

Contents

Concerning Divorce 7
The Most Hateful of all Lawful things 16
The Meaning of Provision 17
Divorce in Islam 20
Two Ways of Divorcing 25
After Divorce 34
Notes 37

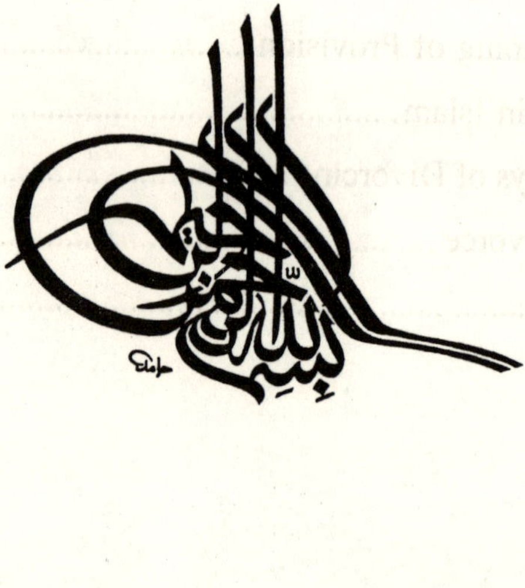
بسم الله الرحمن الرحيم

Concerning Divorce

When a man and a woman bind themselves together by tying the knot of marriage, they cherish the hope of living together for the whole of the rest of their lives. Then, when nature blesses their union with a child, it strengthens the bond of marriage, providing a guarantee of its greater depth and stability. On the basis of data collected in western countries, the *Encyclopaedia Britannica* of 1984 confirms this with the statement that "childless couples tend to have a higher divorce rate than couples with children."[1]

A divorce court judge in the West holds that "every little youngster born to a couple is an added assurance that their marriage will never be dissolved in a divorce court."[2]

Inspite of these apparently favorable psychological factors and natural, traditional attachments of parents and children, the rising incidence of divorce is a new and observable phenomenon of the modern world. One of the most important contributing factors is the ease with which women can now make a living. On this the *Encyclopaedia Britannica* says: "Industrialization has made it easier for women to support themselves, whether they are single, married, divorced, or widowed. In this connection, it is interesting to note that the Great Depression of the 1930s stopped the rise in the number of divorces in the United States for a time."[3]

In the modern age, western civilization has been beset by many problems, many of which are more artificial than real. In many things western civilization has adopted unnatural ways, thus giving rise to unnatural problems. The matter has further been worsened by attempts to solve them unnaturally. Problems have thus gone on increasing instead of decreasing. The problem of divorce is one of them. The initial stimulus of the women's liberation movement in the West was not wrong, but its leaders did not care to define its limits. In a bid to make a free society, their efforts culminated in the creation of a permissive society. Affairs between men and women knew no limits and this had the effect of weakening the marriage bond. Men and women were no more husbands and wives. In the words of the

Prophet, they became sensual, pleasure-seeking people. This state of affairs was given a boost by industrialization, as a woman could easily procure an independent livelihood for herself. This had never before been possible. Because of this, she has frequently refused to live under the guardianship of men which, in consequence has created a large number of social problems leading to greatly increased rates of divorce.

The western philosophers who wanted to check divorce advocated legal curbs upon men, which would legally bind them to provide maintenance to the wife after the divorce. This maintenance sum was fixed according to western living standards, so that, in most cases, divorce meant that the man had to part with a fair amount of his hard earned money for the whole of the rest of his life.

A victim of this unnatural state of affairs was Lord Bertrand Russell, one of the most intelligent and outstanding intellectuals of his time. Soon after his marriage, he discovered that his wife no longer inspired any feelings of love in him. Although realizing this incompatibility, he did not seek an immediate separation. In spite of severe mental torture he tried to bear with this situation for ten years. He refers to this period as one of "darkest despair." Finally he had to separate and remarry, but he was not satisfied even with the second match and he married for a third time. Two divorces were a costly bargain. According to English law, the amount of alimony and maintenance he had to pay his wives upset him greatly. He writes in his Autobiography:

> *... the financial burden was heavy and rather disturbing: I had given Pounds 10,000 of my Nobel Prize cheque for a little more than Pounds 11,000 to my third wife, and I was now paying alimony to her and to my second wife as well as paying for the education of my younger son. Added to this, there were heavy expenses in connection with my elder son's illness; and the income taxes which for many years he had neglected to pay now fell to me to pay.[4]*

Such a law had been passed in order to ensure justice for women who had to resort to divorce. But when people began to realize that divorce inevitably led one into financial straits, the marriage bond began to be dispensed with altogether. Men and women simply started to live together without going through the formality of the marriage ceremony. Now more than fifty percent of the younger generation prefer to live in an unmarried state.

It was only natural that a reaction should have

set in against a law which so patently disfavored men and brought corruption, perversion and all kinds of misery in its wake. Children—even newborn babies—were the greatest sufferers.

Now take the situation prevailing in Hindu society, in which the extreme difficulty of divorce acts as a deterrent. Obviously this was a bid to reform, but this has served only to aggravate the matter. The ancient Indian religious reformers held that separation was illegal: they even prohibited women from remarrying, so that they would be left with no incentive to seek divorce. The laws were made in such a way that once marriage ceremonies were finalized, neither could a man divorce his wife, nor was it possible for a woman to remarry after leaving her former husband.

But such reformations were unnatural, and have been generally detrimental to individuals in Hindu society. When a man and a woman are unable to satisfy one another, the whole of their lives is passed in great bitterness because of there being no provision for remarriage. They are doomed to continue to live a tormented life alongside partners with whom they have nothing in common. I shall cite here only one of the hundreds and thousands of such instances which are reported in newspapers almost everyday, leaving aside those cases which go unreported. Manu, 25, was a cousin of Khushwant Singh. He has written in detail about her tragedy in his "Malice" column.[5] Manu had a flourishing business selling ready-made garments in Los Angeles. As she did not want to marry a foreigner, she decided to come to India to find a husband and return with him to the States. She found her own husband in a tall, handsome, powerfully built Hindu boy who was anxious to go abroad. The marriage took place with all pomp and splendor in a five-star hotel. It took her some months to arrange for her husband's visa, during which time she maintained him and paid for his passage. The marriage was a disaster. The boy turned out to be an alcoholic, prone to violence and averse to doing any work. Manu sought her parent's consent to wind up her business, divorce her husband and return to India. Her parents travelled to America and tried to persuade her not to be hasty. A few days after her mother returned to Delhi, Manu's husband strangled her and dumped her body in a deserted spot. He collected all he could in the house and was planning to flee the United States when the police caught up with him. He is now in jail on a charge of murder.

It is obvious that Manu was not careless in selecting her partner. She travelled from America to find a suitable match in her birth place. But all that glitters is not gold. Our human limitations make it impossible for us to understand every facet of a person's character before entering into a relationship with him. The question arises if, after such revelations, one should feel forced to respect a marriage bond even at the cost of one's life? When society considers separation taboo, or the laws on this show no human leniency, the only alternative left for such incompatible couples is either to commit suicide, or waste away the whole of their lives in the "darkest despair." Even when one dares to surmount the hurdle of divorce, it is very difficult to get remarried in societies where divorcees are looked down upon. One can at best marry someone beneath one's social status. But in Islam remarriage is not a taboo: the Prophet himself married a widow. The provisions of Islam are thus a great blessing to couples who realize only too late that they have erred in making their choice of a partner. Islam provides for them to separate amicably, in a spirit of goodwill.

Just think of couples wasting away the whole of their lives in mental torment only because the conditions of separation and its consequences are hard to meet. It is as unnatural as anything can be.

Islam is a natural religion. Such a situation has not developed in Muslim communities because Islamic law on marriage and divorce provides for all, or almost all, eventualites. For example, when a woman wishes to divorce her husband, she has to put her case before a religious scholar, or a body of religious scholars. This facility is available to her in all the great Arabic schools in India. They then give consideration to her circumstances in the light of the Qur'an and the Hadith, and, if they find that there are reasonable grounds for separation, they decide in her favor. The reason that the woman must have scholars to act on her behalf is that women are more emotional than men—as has been proved by scientific research—and it is to prevent hasty and ill-considered divorces taking place that she is thus advised. If we seldom hear of Muslim women committing suicide, or being murdered by their in-laws, it is because they have the alternative—separation.

Separation, of course, is strongly advised against in the case of minor provocations. Are we not commanded by God to be tolerant and forgiving? It is meant only as a last resort, when it has become truly unavoidable.

Islamic law is thus fair to both husband and wife, unlike occidental law, which places an undue burden on the man, while Hindu society forces the woman into familial rejection, destitution and social ostracism.

The most hateful of all Lawful things

While marriage is the rule of life, and divorce only an exception, the latter must also be accepted as a reality. Indeed there already exist commandments to deal, accordingly, with such cases in both divine and human laws.

The only true, authentic representation of divine law now exists in the form of the Qur'an, it having been preserved in its entirety by God and free, therefore, from all human interpolations. In the Qur'an, and in the Hadith, there are various commandments regarding divorce, the main point being that divorce should be sought only under unavoidable circumstances. The Prophet spoke of it as being the most hateful of all the lawful things in the eyes of God, and said that when it does take place, it should be done in an atmosphere of good will. In no way should one harbor ill-will against the other.[6]

The Meaning of Provision

In Islamic jurisprudence, the material arrangements which a man makes for his divorced spouse are termed "divorce provision." There is a consensus among Muslim scholars that this provision in no way means life-long maintenance, there being absolutely no basis for this in the divine scriptures. The concept of maintenance for life is, in fact, a product of modern civilization. It was never at any time enshrined in divine laws, either in Islam, Judaism or Christianity. In material terms 'provision' simply takes the form of a gift handed over by the man on parting, so that the woman's immediate needs may be catered for, and in all cases, this is quite commensurate with his means.

But the Qur'an makes it explicit that the parting must above all be humane and that justice must be done: "Provide for them with fairness; the rich man according to his means, and the poor according to his. This is binding on righteous men. Do not forget to show kindness to each other... reasonable provision should also be made for divorced women. That is incumbent on righteous men."[7]

When divorce takes place before the settling of the dowry and the consummation of the marriage, even then the man must give the woman money or goods as a gesture of goodwill. In this instance the question of his repaying dowry money does not arise. The Qur'an is also quite explicit on this — "Believers, if you marry believing women and divorce them before the marriage is consummated, you have no right to require them to observe a waiting period. Provide well for them and release them honorably."[8]

This "waiting period" (*iddah*) actually applies to a woman who has been married for some time and who may, subsequent to the divorce, discover that she is pregnant. This statutory waiting period of three months makes her position clear and then the man is required to pay her additional compensation if she is expecting his child. But again there is no question of maintenance for life, for the Qur'an seeks a natural solution to all human problems. It would, therefore, be wholly against the spirit of the Qur'an for a woman to be entitled to life maintenance from the very man with whom she could not co-exist. Such a ruling would surely have created a negative mentality in society. The Qur'an again has the answer: "If they separate, God will compensate each of them out of His own abundance: He is Munificent, Wise."[9]

The munificence of God refers to the vast provision which God has made for his servants in this world.

In various ways God helps such distressed people. For example, when a woman is divorced, it is but natural that the sympathy of all her blood relations should be aroused. And, as a result, without any pressure being put on them, they are willing to help and look after her. Besides, a new will-power is awakened in such a woman and she sets about exploiting her hidden potentialities, thus solving her problems independently. Furthermore, previous experiences having left her wiser and more careful, she feels better equipped to enter into another marital relationship with more success.

Divorce in Islam

Nature demands that men and women lead their lives together. The ideal way of leading such a life is, according to the *shari'ah*, within the bonds of marriage. In Islam, marriage is both a civil contract entered into by mutual consent of the bride and groom, and a highly sacred bond to which great religious and social importance is attached. As an institution, it is a cohesive force in society, and worth protecting and preserving for that reason. To that end, detailed injunctions have been prescribed to maintain its stability and promote its betterment.

However, in the knowledge that an excess of legal constraints can lead to rebellion, such injunctions have been kept to a realistic minimum and have been formulated to be consistent with normal human capabilities. Moreover, their enforcement is less relied upon than the religious conditioning of the individual to ensure the maintenance of high ethical standards and appropriate conduct in marital affairs and family life.

The state of marriage not only lays the foundations for family life, but also provides a training ground for individuals to make a positive adjustment to society. When a man and woman prove to be a good husband and a good wife, they will certainly prove to be good citizens in the broad spectrum of their social group. This has been aptly expressed in a *hadith*: "The best of you is one who is best for his family."[10]

The family being the preliminary unit for the training of human beings, its disintegration has an injurious effect on the society to which those human beings must individually make a positive contribution, if collectively they are to form a good and just nation. If the family no longer exists, it is the whole of humanity which suffers.

Once a man and a woman are tied together in the bonds of matrimony, they are expected to do their utmost, till the day they die to honor and uphold what the Qur'an calls their firm contract, or pledge.[11] To this end, the full thrust of the *shari'ah* is levelled at preventing the occurrence of divorce; the laws it lays down in this regard exist primarily, therefore, as checks, not incentives.

Islam regards marriage as an extremely desirable institution, hence its conception of marriage as the rule of life, and divorce only as an exception to that rule. According to a *hadith*, the Prophet Muhammad said, "Marriage is one of my *sunnah* (way). One who does not follow it does not belong to me."[12]

Although Islam permits divorce, it lays great emphasis on its being a concession, and a measure to be resorted to only when there is no alternative. Seeing it in this light, the Prophet Muhammad said, "Of all things permitted, divorce is the most hateful in the sight of God."[13]

When a man and a woman live together as husband and wife, it is but natural that they should have their differences, it being a biological and psychological fact that each man and each woman born into this world are by their very nature quite different from each other. That is why the sole method of having unity in this world is to live unitedly in spite of differences. This can be achieved only through patience and tolerance, virtues advocated by the Prophet not only in a general sense, but, more importantly, in the particular context of married life. Without these qualities, there can be no stability in the bond of marriage. According to Abu Hurayrah, the Prophet said, "No believing man should bear any grudge against a believing woman. If one of her ways is not to his liking, there must be many things about her that would please him."[14]

It is an accepted fact that everyone has his strengths and his weaknesses, his plus points and his minus points. This is equally true of husbands and wives. In the marital situation, the best policy is for each partner to concentrate on the plus points of the other, while ignoring the minus points. If a husband and wife can see the value of this maxim and consciously adopt it as the main guiding principle in their lives, they will have a far better chance of their marriage remaining stable.

However, it sometimes happens, with or without reason, that unpleasantness crops up, and goes on increasing between husband and wife, with no apparent indication of their being able to smooth things out by themsleves. Their thinking about each other in a way that is conditioned by their maladjustment prevents them from arriving at a just settlement of their differences, based on facts rather than on opinions. In such a case, the best strategy according to the Qur'an is to introduce a third party who will act as an arbiter. Not having any previous association with the matters under dispute, he will remain dispassionate and will be able to arrive at an objective decision acceptable to both parties.

For any arbiter to be successful, however, the husband and wife must also adopt the correct attitude.

Here is an incident from the period of the four pious Caliphs which will illustrate this point.

When 'Ali ibn Abi Talib reigned as fourth Caliph, a married couple complaining of marital discord came to him to request a settlement. In the light of the above-mentioned Qur'anic guidance 'Ali ordered that a board of arbiters, one from the husband's family and one from the wife's family, be set up, which should make proper enquiries into the circumstances and then give its verdict. This verdict was to be accepted without argument by both sides.

As recorded in the book, *Jami' al-Bayan*, by at-Tabari, the woman said that she gave her consent, on the book of God, whether the verdict was for or against her. But the man protested that he would not accept the verdict if it was for separation. 'Ali said, "What you say is improper. By God, you cannot move from here until you have shown your willingness to accept the verdict of the arbiters in the same spirit as the woman has shown."

This makes it clear that a true believer should wholeheartedly accept the arbiters and their verdict in accordance with the Qur'anic injunctions. Once their verdict is given, there should be no further dispute.

Two Ways of Divorcing

However, it has to be conceded that life does not always function smoothly, like a machine. Despite all safeguards, it sometimes does happen that a couple reaches a stage of such desperation that they become intent on separation. Here the *shari'ah* gives them guidance in that it prescribes a specific method for separation. The Qur'an expresses it thus: "Divorce may be pronounced twice, then a woman must be retained in honor or allowed to go with kindness."[15]

This verse has been interpreted to mean that a man who has twice given notice of divorce over a period of two months should remember God before giving notice a third time. Then he should either keep his spouse with him in a spirit of goodwill, or he should release her without doing her any injustice.

This method of divorce prescribed by the Qur'an, i.e. taking three months to finalize it, makes it impossible for a man seeking divorce suddenly to cast his wife aside. Once he has said to his wife (who should not at this time be menstruating), "I divorce you," both are expected to think the situation over for a whole month. If the man has a change of opinion during this period, he can withdraw his words. If not, he will again say, "I divorce you," (again his wife should be in a state of "purity") and they must again review the situation for a further month. Even at this stage, the husband has the right to revoke the proceedings if he has had a change of heart. If, however, in the third month, he says, "I divorce you," the divorce becomes final and the man ceases to have any right to revoke it. Now he is obliged to part with his wife in a spirit of good will, and give her full rights.

This prescribed method of divorce has ensured that it is a well-considered, planned arrangement and not just a rash step taken in a fit of emotion. When we remember that in most cases, divorce is the result of a fit of anger, we realize that the prescribed method places a tremendous curb on divorce. It takes into account the fact that anger never lasts—tempers necessarily cool down after some time—and that those who feel like divorcing their wives in a fit of anger will certainly repent their emotional outburst and will wish to withdraw from the position it has put them in. It also takes into account the fact that divorce is a not a simple matter: it amounts to the breaking up of the home and destroying the children's future. It is only when tempers have cooled down that the dire consequences of divorce are realized, and the necessity to revoke the decision becomes clear.

When a man marries a woman, he has to say only once that he accepts her as his spouse. But for divorce, the Qur'an enjoins a three month period for it to be finalized. That is, for marriage, one utterance is enough, but for a divorce to be finalized, three utterances are required, between which a long gap has been prescribed by the *shari'ah*. The purpose of this gap is to give the husband sufficient time to revise his decision, and to consult the well-wishers around him. It also allows time for relatives to intervene in the hopes of persuading both husband and wife to avoid a divorce. Without this gap, none of these things could be achieved. That is why divorce proceedings have to be spread out over a long period of time.

All these preventive measures clearly allow frayed tempers to cool, so that the divorce proceedings need not reach a stage which is irreversible. Divorce, after all, has no saving graces, particularly in respect of its consequences. It simply amounts to ridding oneself of one set of problems only to become embroiled in another set of problems.

Despite all such preventive measures, it does sometimes happen that a man acts in ignorance, or is rendered incapable of thinking coolly by a fit of anger. Then on a single occasion, in a burst of temper, he utters the word "divorce" three times in a row, *"talaq, talaq, talaq!"* Such incidents, which took place in the Prophet's lifetime, still take place even today. Now the question arises as to how the would-be divorcer should be treated. Should his three utterances of *talaq* be treated as only one, and should he then be asked to extend his decision over a three-month period? Or should his three utterances of *talaq* on a single occasion be equated with the three utterances of *talaq* made separately over a three-month period? There is a *hadith* recorded by Imam Abu Dawud and several other traditionists which can give us guidance in this matter: Rukana ibn Abu Yazid said *"talaq"* to his wife three times on a single occasion. Then he was extremely sad at the step he had taken. The Prophet asked him exactly how he had divorced her. He replied that he had said *"talaq"* to her three times in a row. The Prophet then observed, "All three count as only one. If you want, you may revoke it."[16]

A man may say *"talaq"* to his wife three times in a row, in contravention of the *shari'ah*'s prescribed method, thereby committing a sin, but if he was known to be in an emotionally overwrought state at the time his act may be considered a mere absurdity arising from human weakness. His three utterances of the word *talaq* may be taken as an expression of the intensity of his emotions and thus the equivalent of only one such utterance. He is likely to be told that, having transgressed a *shari'ah* law, he must seek God's forgiveness, must regard his three utterances as only one, and must take a full three months to arrive at his final decision.

In the first phase of Islam, however, a different view of divorce was taken by the second Caliph, 'Umar ibn al-Khattab. An incident which illustrates his viewpoint was thus described by Imam Muslim.

In the Prophet's lifetime, then under the Caliphate of Abu Bakr and also during the early period of the Caliphate of 'Umar, three utterances of *talaq* on one occasion used to be taken together as only one utterance. Then it occurred to 'Umar ibn al-Khattab that in spite of the fact that a system had been laid down which permitted the husband to withdraw his first, or even second *talaq*, men still wanted to rush into divorce. He felt that if they were bent on being hasty, why should not a rule be imposed on them binding them to a final divorce on the utterance of *talaq* three times in a row. And he proceeded to impose such a rule.

This act on the part of the second Caliph, apparently against the principles of the Qur'an and *sunnah*, did not in any way change the law of the *shari'ah*. To think that this led to any revision of Islamic law would be to misunderstand the situation: the Caliph's order merely constituted an exception to the rule, and was, moreover, of a temporary nature. This aptly demonstrates how the Islamic *shari'ah* may make concessions in accordance with circumstances.

Each law of the *shari'ah* may be eternal, but a Muslim ruler has the power to make exceptions in the case of certain individuals in special sets of circumstances. However, such a ruling will not take on the aspect of an eternal law. It will be purely temporary in nature and duration.

Various traditions in this connection show that the second Caliph's treatment of certain persons was not in consonance with the *shari'ah*. The rulings he gave on these occasions were in the nature of executive orders which were consistent with his position as a ruler. If he acted in this manner, it was to punish those who were being hasty in finalizing the divorce procedure.

It is a matter of Islamic historical record that when any such person was brought before 'Umar for having uttered the word *talaq* three times on one occasion, he held this to be rebellious conduct and would order him to be flogged on the back.[17]

Perhaps the most important aspect of this matter is that when 'Umar gave his exceptional verdict on divorce being final after the third utterance on a single occasion of the word *talaq*, his position was not that of a powerless *'alim* (scholar) but of a ruler invested with the full power to punish—as a preventive measure—anyone who went against Qur'anic injunctions. This was to discourage haste in divorce. By accepting a man's three *talaqs* on the one occasion as final and irrevocable, he caused him to forfeit his right to revoke his initial decision, thus leaving him with no option but to proceed with the divorce.

On the other hand, the Caliph had it in his power to fully compensate any woman affected by this ruling. For instance, he was in a position to guarantee her an honorable life in society and if, due to being divorced, she was in need of financial assistance, he could provide her with continuing maintenance from the government exchequer, *baitul mal*, etc.

Today, anyone who cites 'Umar's ruling as a precedent in order to justify the finality of a divorce based on three utterances of the word *talaq* on a single occasion should remember that his verdict will remain unenforceable for the simple reason that he does not have the powers that 'Umar, as Caliph, possessed. 'Umar's verdict was that of a powerful ruler of the time and not just that of a common man. It is necessary at this point to clear certain misunderstandings which have arisen about the extent of agreement which existed on 'Umar's ruling. Of all the Prophet's Companions who were present at Medina at that time, perhaps the only one to disagree was 'Ali. As a result of this, certain *'ulama* have come to the conclusion that the Prophet's followers (*Sahabah*) had reached a consensus (*'ijma*) on this matter.[18]

But the consensus reached was not on the general issue of divorce, but on the right of Muslim rulers to make temporary and exceptional rulings, as had been done by 'Umar. It is obvious that the Companions of the Prophet could never have agreed to annul a Qur'anic injunction or to modify for all time to come a prescribed system of divorce. All that was agreed upon was that exceptional circumstances warranted exceptional rulings on the part of the Caliph. He was entitled to punish in any manner he thought fitting, anyone who digressed from the *shari'ah*. This right possessed by the ruler of the time is clearly established in the *shari'ah*. Many other instances, not necessarily relating to personal disputes, can be cited of his exercise of this right.

After Divorce

The question that arises immediately after divorce is of ways and means to meet one's necessary expenses. One's answer is to resort to the Islamic law of inheritance. If women were to be given their due share according to Islamic law, there would be no question of a woman becoming destitute. But, sad to say, the majority of Muslim women fail to get their due share of inheritance from their deceased fathers and husbands as stipulated by Islamic law. If they could do so, this would be more than enough to meet such emergencies.

However, Islam has not just left women's financial problems to the vagaries of inheritance, because parents are not invariably in possession of property which can be divided among their children. Further arrangements have been made under the maintenance law, but this has no connection with the law of divorce. The answer to this question must be sought therefore in the Islamic law of maintenance. Here we shall briefly describe some of its aspects:

1. In case the divorced woman is childless or the chidren are not earning, according to Islamic law, the responsibility for her maintenance falls on her father. That is, her situation will be the same as it was before marriage.

To quote from *Fath al-Qadir*[19]:

The Father is responsible for bearing the expenses of his daughter till her marriage, in the event of her having no money. The father has no right to force her to earn, even if she is able to. When the girl is divorced and the period of confinement is over, her father shall again have to bear her expenses.[20]

2. If the divorced woman has a son who is an earning member of the family, the responsibility for her maintenance falls entirely upon him.

All that rightfully belongs to a wife, will be the duty of the son to provide, that is, food, drink, clothes, house and even servants, if possible.[21]

3. In the case of the father being deceased, and where even her children are unable to earn, her nearest relatives such as brothers or uncles are responsible for her upkeep. In the absence of even this third form, the Islamic *shari'ah* holds the State Treasury (*baitul mal*) responsible for bearing her expenses. She will be entitled to receive the money for her necessities.

Because of the number of provisions made under Islamic law for women it has never been the case in Islamic history that Muslim divorced women have been cast adrift, helpless, with no one to look after them.

Indian columnist, Khushwant Singh has remarked that we do not hear of Muslim women committing suicide or being tortured like Hindu women, which is a proof that Islam has already given them adequate liberty and has made enough provision for them to be supported in times of emergencies.

A new dimension has been added to the issue since the women of this day and age can leave their homes to work, and are therefore not as entirely dependent on men as they used to be in the past: there is no need then to make laws which provide for them at the expense of their menfolk. When they are earning like men, what is the point in making such a law? Only in exceptional cases, surely, do they need to be looked after, and ways and means of doing so can generally be worked out quite satisfactorily on a personal level.

Notes

1. *Encyclopaedia Britannica* (1984), vol. 7, pp. 163-164.
2. Ibid.
3. Ibid.
4. Bertrand Russell, *Autobiography,* (London, 1978), pp. 563-564.
5. *The Hindustan Times*, (New Delhi), October 12, 1985.
6. Abu Dawud, *Sunan, Kitab at-Talaq*, 2/255.
7. Qur'an, 2:236.
8. Qur'an, 33:49.
9. Qur'an, 4:130.
10. Ibn Majah, *Sunan, Kitab an-Nikah*, 1/636.
11. Qur'an, 4:21.
12. Ibn Majah, *Sunan, Kitab an-Nikah*.
13. Abu Dawud, *Sunan, Kitab at-Talaq*, 2/255.
14. Muslim, *Sahih, Kitab ar-Rada'*, 2/1091.
15. Qur'an, 2:229.
16. *Fath al-Bari*, 9/275.
17. *Fath al-Bari*, 9/275.
18. *Rawai' al-Bayan*, 1/334.
19. A standard book on Islamic Law.
20. Al-Shaokani, *Fath al-Qadir*, 3/344.
21. Ibn 'Abidin, *Radd al-Muhtar 'ala ad-Durr al-Mukhtar*, 2/733.

Goodword English Publications

The Holy Quran: Text, Translation and Commentary (HB), Tr. Abdullah Yusuf Ali

The Holy Quran (PB), Tr. Abdullah Yusuf Ali

The Holy Quran (Laminated Board), Tr. Abdullah Yusuf Ali

The Holy Quran (HB), Tr. Abdullah Yusuf Ali

Holy Quran (Small Size), Tr. Abdullah Yusuf Ali

The Quran, Tr. T.B. Irving

The Koran, Tr. M.H. Shakir

The Glorious Quran, Tr. M.M. Pickthall

Allah is Known Through Reason, Harun Yahya

The Basic Concepts in the Quran, Harun Yahya

Crude Understanding of Disbelief, Harun Yahya

Darwinism Refuted, Harun Yahya

Death Resurrection Hell, Harun Yahya

Devoted to Allah, Harun Yahya

Eternity Has Already Begun, Harun Yahya

Ever Thought About the Truth?, Harun Yahya

The Mercy of Believers, Harun Yahya

The Miracle in the Ant, Harun Yahya

The Miracle in the Immune System, Harun Yahya

The Miracle of Man's Creation, Harun Yahya

The Miracle of Hormones, Harun Yahya

The Miracle in the Spider, Harun Yahya

The Miracle of Creation in DNA, Harun Yahya

The Miracle of Creation in Plants, Harun Yahya

The Moral Values of the Quran, Harun Yahya

The Nightmare of Disbelief, Harun Yahya

Perfected Faith, Harun Yahya

Bouquet of the Noble Hadith, Assad Nimer Busool

Forty Hadith, Assad Nimer Busool

Hijrah in Islam, Dr. Zafarul Islam Khan

Palestine Documents, Dr. Zafarul Islam Khan

At the Threshold of New Millennium, Dr. Zafarul Islam Khan

Islamic Sciences, Waqar Husaini

Islamic Thought..., Waqar Husaini

The Qur'an for Astronomy, Waqar Husaini

A Dictionary of Muslim Names, Prof. S.A. Rahman

Let's Speak Arabic, Prof. S.A. Rahman

Teach Yourself Arabic, Prof. S.A. Rahman

Islamic Medicine, Edward G. Browne

Literary History of Persia (Vol.1 & 2), Edward G. Browne

Literary History of Persia (Vol.3 & 4), Edward G. Browne

The Soul of the Quran, Saniyasnain Khan

Presenting the Quran, Saniyasnain Khan

The Wonderful Universe of Allah, Saniyasnain Khan

A-Z Ready Reference of the Quran (Based on the Translation by Abdullah Yusuf Ali), Mohammad Imran Erfani

The Alhambra, Washington Irving

The Encyclopaedic Index of the Quran, Dr. Syed Muhammad Osama

The Essentials of Islam, Al-Haj Saeed Bin Ahmed Al Lootah

Glossary of the Quran, Aurang Zeb Azmi

Introducing Arabic, Michael Mumisa

Arabic-English Dictionary, J.G. Hava

The Arabs in History, Prof. Bernard Lewis

A Basic Reader for the Holy Quran, Syed Mahmood Hasan

The Beauty of Makkah and Madinah, Mohamed Amin

A Brief Illustrated Guide to Understanding Islam, I.A. Ibrahim

The Concept of Society in Islam and Prayersin Islam, Dr. Syed Abdul Latif

Decisive Moments in the History of Islam, Muhammad Abdullah Enan

The Handy Concordance of the Quran, Aurang Zeb Azmi

Quick Grasp of Faith, Harun Yahya

Timelessness and the Reality of Fate, Harun Yahya

In Search of God, Maulana Wahiduddin Khan

Islam and Peace, Maulana Wahiduddin Khan

An Islamic Treasury of Virtues, Maulana Wahiduddin Khan

The Moral Vision, Maulana Wahiduddin Khan

Muhammad: A Prophet for All Humanity, Maulana Wahiduddin Khan

Principles of Islam, Maulana Wahiduddin Khan

Prophet Muhammad : A Simple Guide to His Life, Maulana Wahiduddin Khan

The Quran for All Humanity, Maulana Wahiduddin Khan

The Quran: An Abiding Wonder, Maulana Wahiduddin Khan

Religion and Science, Maulana Wahiduddin Khan

Simple Wisdom (HB), Maulana Wahiduddin Khan

Simple Wisdom (PB), Maulana Wahiduddin Khan

The True Jihad, Maulana Wahiduddin Khan

Tabligh Movement, Maulana Wahiduddin Khan

A Treasury of the Quran, Maulana Wahiduddin Khan

Woman Between Islam and Western Society, Maulana Wahiduddin Khan

Woman in Islamic Shari'ah, Maulana Wahiduddin Khan

The Ideology of Peace, Maulana Wahiduddin Khan

Indian Muslims, Maulana Wahiduddin Khan

Introducing Islam, Maulana Wahiduddin Khan

Islam: Creator of the Modern Age, Maulana Wahiduddin Khan

Islam: The Voice of Human Nature, Maulana Wahiduddin Khan

Islam Rediscovered, Maulana Wahiduddin Khan

Words of the Prophet Muhammad, Maulana Wahiduddin Khan

God Arises, Maulana Wahiduddin Khan

The Call of the Qur'an, Maulana Wahiduddin Khan

Building a Strong and Prosperous India and Role of Muslims, Maulana Wahiduddin Khan

Islam As It Is, Maulana Wahiduddin Khan

Sermons of the Prophet Muhammad, Assad Nimer Busool